THE ILLUSTRATED WORLD OF

THE
TUDORS

Peter Chrisp

illustrated by
Adam Hook

WAYLAND

Also available:
The Illustrated World of the Victorians

© Copyright 2000 Wayland

Published in Great Britain in 2000 by Hodder Wayland,
an imprint of Hodder Children's Books
Reprinted in 2003 and 2004
Reprinted in 2006 by Wayland, an imprint of Hachette Children's Books

Editor: Philippa Smith
Designer: Sharon Hugshe

A Catalogue record for this book is available from
the British Library.

ISBN-10: 0 7502 2614 5
ISBN-13: 978 0 7502 2614 1

Printed and bound in China

Hachette Children's Books
338 Euston Road, London NW1 3BH

Contents

Words that appear in **bold** in the text are
explained in the glossary on page 30.

Tudor Times

More than four hundred years ago, England was ruled by a family of kings and queens called the Tudors. Let's travel back to the 1500s, and see what it was like to live in Tudor times.

▼ *England's biggest town was London, which you can see here.*

All English people were Christian. By law, they were supposed to go to church every Sunday and on special religious 'holy days', when no work was done. This is where we get our word 'holiday'.

▼ *Religion was very important. Look at all the church towers.*

Beggars and Thieves

In Tudor times, life was very hard for poor people. Many could not find work, and had to beg or steal to live.

People kept their money in purses, which hung by strings from their belts. Thieves called **cutpurses** would cut the strings to steal the purse.

▲ A pickpocket counts the money he has stolen.

◀ A boy is taught to steal by an older thief. He must get the coins without ringing the bells on the purse.

▼ *A card cheat invites you to play a game.*

Some men had more clever ways of getting hold of money. There were many tricksters. They would trick people by cheating at games of cards or dice, played for money.

By law, only the disabled, or those too old to work, were allowed to beg. They were given tin badges showing that they had this right. Some healthy beggars tried to get round the law by pretending to be ill.

▶ *This beggar has just rubbed his arms with poisonous plants, to make nasty sores appear.*

Painful Punishments

 In Tudor times, punishments for crime were harsh. People caught stealing even small sums of money could be hanged – killed with a rope around their necks.

Hanging was only one of the many painful punishments. You could also be whipped, or have your hands cut off.

In 1579, a man called John Stubbs wrote a book which upset Queen Elizabeth. He was sentenced to have his right hand chopped off. After this was done, he raised his hat with his left hand, cried 'God save the Queen!' and fainted.

▼ *The hangman gets his rope ready.*

For less serious crimes, you could be locked in the stocks. This was a wooden frame fixed over the legs. You had to spend all day sitting like this, while people made fun of you and pelted you with rubbish.

▼ Imagine having to sit in the stocks all day!

People were always locked in the stocks on market day, the day when towns were crowded with men and women buying and selling goods. This meant that there were plenty of people around to throw the rubbish.

Dangerous Streets

Tudor towns could be dangerous places. In any dark street you might meet a **footpad**, a thief who would attack you to steal your money. Men carried swords and daggers to defend themselves.

▼ *In this street, a footpad has just knocked someone out, while a cutpurse is about to steal a purse. Can you find them?*

Dangers of Disease

Towns were filthy, smelly and full of rubbish. People lived alongside rats and fleas. Bites from rat fleas spread a terrible disease called the **plague**. (How many rats can you find in this book?)

In 1563, 17,404 Londoners died of the plague. This was one person in every six who lived there.

▲ *This sick-looking man has just caught the plague.*

Tudor doctors did not understand the true causes of most diseases. Many wrongly thought that the plague was carried in the air.

Doctors believed that illnesses were often caused by having too much 'bad blood'. They would get rid of this blood by cutting their patients, or by sticking blood-sucking worms, called leeches, on them.

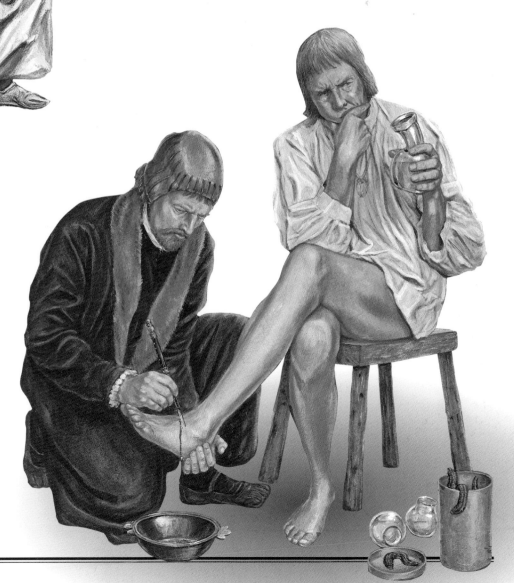

▲ This doctor wears a mask stuffed with sweet-smelling herbs, to protect him from the air.

▶ A doctor lets blood with a knife. His wriggling leeches wait for their next meal.

Curious Cures

If you were sick, you could buy medicine from an **apothecary**. He made medicines from all sorts of funny things, including spiders' webs, woodlice and mice!

Mice were used in several ways. Their bones were ground up with honey and roses to make medicine for earache. They were cut in half and rubbed on the feet of people with **gout**. They were also served fried to cure whooping cough.

▲ *An apothecary gets ready to grind up a mouse for medicine.*

▶ *Burning a candle to cure toothache.*

A candle was used for toothache, which was wrongly thought to be caused by tiny worms. The smoke was supposed to make the worms drop out.

▼ *Passing a baby over a donkey, to cure her cough.*

Rather than pay for a doctor or an apothecary, many people treated themselves when they were sick. They used 'folk cures' – cures invented and passed on by ordinary people.

Folk cures were often thought up because they reminded people of an illness. A donkey makes a 'hee-haw' sound, like a cough. This gave somebody the idea that donkeys could cure coughs!

The Playhouse

 The most popular London entertainment was the 'playhouse' or theatre. Playhouses were round buildings, open to the sky. Each playhouse had room for about 2,500 people in the audience.

▼ *Actors often made speeches to the audience. Such speeches are called 'soliloquies'.*

▲ *London's Globe Theatre, built in 1599.*

All sorts of people visited the playhouse. Poor people paid a small sum to stand in the yard around the stage. They were nicknamed 'groundlings' because they stood on the ground.

Richer people paid more to sit on comfortable seats in the balconies. They liked to show off their expensive and fashionable clothes.

▶ *A richly dressed couple take their seats.*

The Show

 Playhouses offered something for everyone. There were comedies – happy plays full of jokes, music and dance. There were also serious plays, called tragedies, with unhappy endings.

Plays were written in verse, like poetry, and people who liked poems enjoyed listening to the words.

◀ *A clown playing a pipe and drum in a comedy.*

Clowns, such as Richard Tarlton and Will Kemp, were huge stars. Their jokes were printed in books, and pictures of them were sold as **souvenirs**.

◀ *Skulls were used in some tragedies, to make the audience think about death.*

Playhouse audiences drank beer and ate apples. If the groundlings got bored with a play, they threw their apples at the actors.

▼ *A fashionable young man buys an apple.*

Action Scenes

Plays had lots of exciting action scenes to keep the crowd entertained. There were sword fights with real weapons. Actors wore bags of pig's blood, which burst in a fight, making it look as if they really had been stabbed.

There were gruesome scenes showing characters being put to death. In one play, three actors wore false stomachs, filled with sheep livers, lungs and hearts. Another actor sliced their stomachs open, stuck his hands inside, and pulled out the bloody organs.

▲ *An actor puts on a bag of pig's blood, before a fight scene.*

On the stage there was a trapdoor, which was used by actors playing ghosts and devils. They would jump up through the trapdoor, and give the audience a big surprise.

▶ An actor playing a devil leaps onto the stage holding a firework. Just behind him, a man plays a roll on his drum.

Fire!

One of the biggest dangers of living in towns came from fires. Most buildings were made of wood, which burns very easily. There was no fire brigade to come to the rescue if a fire started.

The Globe Theatre had a roof of straw, which burns even more quickly than wood. In 1613, the roof caught fire when a cannon was fired during a show. The theatre burned to the ground but, luckily, nobody was hurt.

▼ *Straw on a roof is called 'thatch'. This thatcher is fastening the straw to the roof with bent sticks.*

▲ The audience rush from the exits, as flames race through the Globe Theatre.

▶ One man's clothes caught fire. He put the flames out by pouring beer over himself.

Going to Sea

In 1585, England went to war with Spain. The war was mostly fought at sea, so the English **Navy** needed ships and sailors. Some men were happy to go to sea. Others were 'pressed', or forced to become sailors.

Ship's crews included boys as young as twelve.

◀ *Once you were at sea, you had to obey orders. Sailors who did not do this were beaten.*

▼ *Loading supplies on to a warship, before going to sea.*

Dangers of the Sea

 It was much harder to find your way at sea than it is today. The risks of a long voyage were of getting lost at sea, or being shipwrecked.

Hundreds of Tudor shipwrecks still lie on the sea-bed around the British Isles. Most of the ships ran aground on rocks, or were sunk during stormy weather.

*◄ The captain tries to work out where he is going by looking at a map. The round object is a **compass**, showing him the direction in which his ship is sailing.*

Sea battles were fought with cannon – big guns which fired stone or metal balls at enemy ships.

During a battle, a warship was a terrible place to be. Enemy cannon balls smashed into the ship, toppling masts, and sending razor-sharp wooden splinters flying through the air. Battles were noisy, smoky and very scary!

▼ *The ship's boy brings gunpowder to fire the cannon.*

Life at Sea

 There was always plenty of work to be done on a ship. Strong winds and enemy cannon balls could break ropes and rip sails, which often needed mending.

The main food was meat, salted to stop it going rotten, and hard dry biscuits. This was horrible to eat. The lack of fresh food, such as fruit, made many sailors fall sick from a disease called **scurvy**.

▲ *The ship's boy mends a sail.*

In twenty years, around 10,000 sailors died of scurvy. More sailors were killed by the food than in sea battles.

◄ *Even at sea you couldn't escape from rats, which often got at the ship's biscuits.*

Life on a ship could be very boring. Sailors might spend months at sea, with nothing to do but work, sleep and make their own entertainment.

Now you've seen what life was like in Tudor times, on land and at sea. Would you like to have lived then instead of now?

▲ *Sailors slept in* **hammocks** *which swung from side to side as the ship rocked.*

▶ *In their free time, the sailors danced to fiddle music.*

Glossary

apothecary   A kind of doctor, who made and sold medicines.

compass   An instrument with a needle that points to the north. Sailors used a compass to find their way at sea.

cutpurse   A thief who stole purses by cutting their strings.

footpad   A thief on foot, who attacked and robbed people.

gout   A disease which makes the joints swell up, especially the big toe.

hammock   A long piece of strong cloth with ropes at each end, used as a bed on a ship.

Navy   Ships and sailors serving their country, fighting the enemy in wartime.

plague   A deadly disease spread by bites from rat fleas.

scurvy   A disease caused by the lack of fresh food, especially fruit and vegetables.

souvenirs   Things people keep to remind them of a special occasion, such as a holiday, or a trip to the theatre.

Book to Read

Daily Life in a Tudor House by Laura Wilson (Heinemann, 1995)
History Journeys: A Tudor Journey by Philip Steele (Hodder Wayland, 2004)
History Starts Here: The Tudors by Fiona Reynoldson (Hodder Wayland, 1999)
You Wouldn't Want To Be Ill in Tudor Times! by Kathryn Senior
  (Hodder Wayland, 2002)

Places to Visit

The Globe Theatre, Bankside, London
(tel: 0207 401 9919)
Reconstruction of the famous playhouse

Hampton Court Palace, Kingston, Surrey
(tel: 0870 752 7777)
A magnificent Tudor palace, with wonderfully restored kitchens.

Hardwick Hall, Chesterfield, Derbyshire
(tel: 01246 850430)
A beautiful Tudor house, built in the 1590s.

Kentwell Hall, Long Melford, Suffolk
(tel: 01787 310207)
A large Tudor house, where feasts and other Tudor events are staged.

The Mary Rose Museum, Royal Naval Base, Portsmouth
(tel: 0239 275 0521)
Visit the wreck of a Tudor warship, sunk in 1545.

Index